Preface

Most of us believe that if we could just *make* more money, we would *have* more money, but reality proves differently. There does not seem to be a direct correlation between *making* more money and *having* more money. Why? Because we always figure out a way to spend everything we make! In other words, the more we make, the more we spend, and the more we make and spend, the more our debt increases!

My experience reveals that "having money" depends more so on how much we *manage* money than on how much we *make* money. Money management is not a skill that we inherit at birth. It is a learned ability that can be cultivated if we have a little desire and determination. That learning experience must include learning how to manage our credit as well as our cash.

Thus, the need for a short, easy-to-read booklet which will share some proven principles about handling our cash and our credit. The principles shared herein are based on three sources: (1) Personal experience, (2) Patterns that I have seen in the lives of countless clients, and (3) Plain old common sense.

I am a teacher, but I am also a student, so I do not have all the answers. I simply have stumbled on a few answers that might serve to be of help to you like they were to me.

So, let's learn together as we discuss "How To Have Money With The Money You Have."

Jim Garnett

HOW TO HAVE MONEY
WITH THE MONEY YOU HAVE

Section One: CREDIT CARDS

Three Common Mistakes People Make With Credit Cards

Section Two: CASH

A Four-Step Approach To Setting Up A Workable Budget

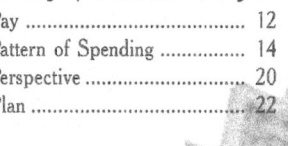

SECTION ONE:
CREDIT CARDS

There are many things in life that are not intrinsically good or bad. How they affect our lives depends upon how we use them. Credit cards are a good example of this. They are not good or bad in themselves, but they can certainly affect our lives for the good or bad, depending upon how they are used.

A credit card can allow us, for example, to take advantage of a sale and actually save money on something we were planning on buying later. A credit card can allow us to avoid carrying larger amounts of cash with us if safety is a factor. A credit card can be used to reserve hotel rooms or rental cars as we travel. They enable us to "have now and pay later," and this is OK in many situations. They also enable us to make repairs or replacements immediately on such things as cars or appliances. And credit cards often offer special "perks" for using them like discounts, cash back, flyer miles, etc. To be sure, credit cards can be a major convenience for us.

BUT credit cards are not always our friends. They can become our foes if we do not understand what they are and how to use them. I am not advocating that you should fear them or avoid them. I just want to instill within you a healthy dose of respect for them. My clients, who average about $16,000 of credit card debt, could share with you how credit cards became their worst nightmares! If we misuse them, they will impact our lives negatively for many years to come.

In observing the experiences of hundreds of new clients each month, I have seen a pattern of three common mistakes they have made in their use of credit cards. These mistakes are made with little reference to age or

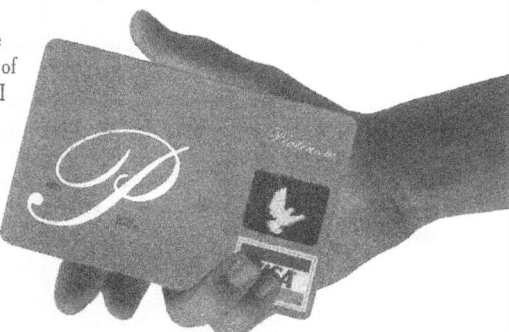

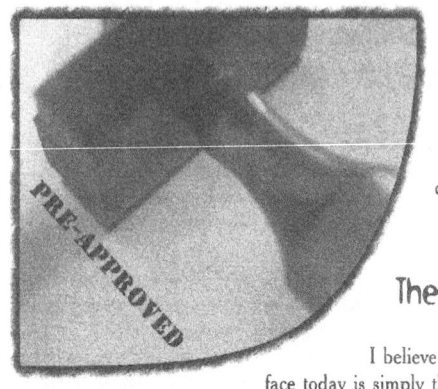

social status. It is a good practice to try to learn from the mistakes of others. It is like learning from "the school of hard knocks" without actually going to class!

Mistake #1:
The Potential We Enjoy

I believe that part of the problem we face today is simply that credit is so easy to get, perhaps too easy. The POTENTIAL that you and I have of getting credit is astounding! We have access today to four times as much credit on credit cards as we did 10 years ago. Access to credit on credit cards has increased from having five available cards with $2,000 credit limits each, to 10 available cards with $4,000 credit limits on each! Our salaries have not kept up with that rate of increase, so we have more credit available with less ability to repay it! With credit so accessible one would expect to find a number of people over-extended in debt ... and we do! A LOT of people.

The credit card industry entices us with TV and radio ads, plus they mail out more than 3 BILLION SOLICITATIONS every year to prospective new customers. That averages 25 offers per year for every family in America! I wonder how big a stack we would have if we saved all these offers for a year.

And the poor college students! They tell me they are deluged with credit card offers when they go off to school. On the phone, in the mail, in the lunch-room, between classes, even under the dorm doors at night! Credit card offers are literally everywhere for their taking! It is not unusual for an 18-year old college freshman to have access to 10-20 different credit cards the very first week of college.

With this much advertising, one would be tempted to conclude that there are BIG BUCKS to be made in the credit card business. That would be a pretty good assumption. Today's average card carrier has 6-7 active cards, a $1,600 balance on each, and pays an interest rate of around 18.3 percent. Only a little over half of all cardholders pay off their balances in full each month. All the rest pay finance charges. That would amount to quite a profit for the credit card industry when you consider that more than $1 TRILLION was charged on cards last year! The average consumer will spend 34% more every time he uses his credit card as opposed to using cash or check! No wonder those merchants love to see us pulling out our cards at the malls.

People have more access to credit than they need. The problem arises from the fact that most people will spend what they have access to spend, whether it is cash or credit. If we have a way to get what we "want," the "want" quickly becomes a "need." We must assume the responsibility to not over-use credit just because the potential to do so is there!

Each of us is ultimately responsible for our use of credit! Just because it is so freely offered does not mean we have to avail ourselves of it. It is not forced upon us. We have a choice!

The POTENTIAL for getting credit today is simply amazing! The temptation to overuse and abuse it is great. That is the way things are and we must prepare ourselves for the deluge of credit offers. Understanding what credit is, we must exercise caution and wisdom in using it. And this leads us to the second mistake people make.

Mistake #2:
The Perception We Use

When I speak to high school or college students, I usually take a jar of cut up credit cards with me and set it at the front of the room. I ask the students to figure out how much money is in the jar if there are 300 cards in it, and each has a $4,000 credit limit. Before long someone will give me the standard answer of $1,200,000, and I will say, "No, that is incorrect." After a few moments of the students assuring me that that is the correct answer, I will tell them it was a

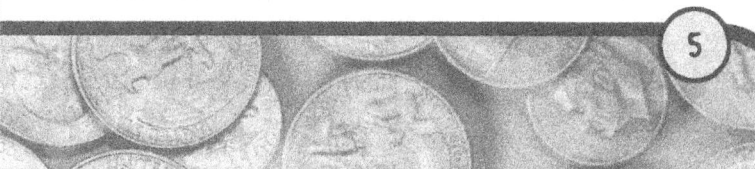

trick question asked to prove a point. The actual answer in that there is NO MONEY in the jar! Credit cards are NOT money, they are DEBT! I figure that if they remember only that, I will have been a success in helping them.

Yes, our PERSPECTIVE toward credit cards is wrong. We tend to see them as money, cash, or wealth, when in essence their buying power is no different than taking out a loan each time we use them. They create debt for us.

CREDIT CARDS ≠ $

I worked with a young man who would boast that he had five credit cards with high limits on each one. He felt that the cards gave him "money in his pocket!" You'd often find him picking up the tab for his friends as he "shared his wealth." He thought his "credit dollars" were like real dollars, but they were not! The last time I saw him he told me that he had maxed out every single card, and learned the hard way that having credit cards does not equal having money. Their buying power simply creates the opportunity to go into debt.

Credit card usage is unlike any other type of debt we incur. The payment is a "detached" payment, in that there is little visual or mental registering that a debt has occurred. There is no deduction to record in our checkbook ledger, and no change to put back into our billfold. There is no visual transaction that trips a mental lever to tell us we have just created a debt. It is almost as though we have spent money without spending money!

That is probably why the husband answered me the way he did the other day. I asked the couple, "How much did you spend on Christmas last year?" The man looked at his wife, then answered, "We didn't spend anything for Christmas, did we honey, we put it on credit cards." His statement would have been funny if that indeed had not actually been his perception. He was not joking.

It is very important to understand this: Each time you use a credit card, you are creating DEBT for yourself. It may not seem like it, but it is so. The bill will eventually come due and you will be required to pay "real money" for what

6

you have purchased. The card's buying power makes it seem like you are spending money, but you are not. "Credit dollars" are not dollars at all, they are simply debt.

So, expect the deluge of card offers. Anticipate that you will have ample opportunity to get cards, but remember what they ARE and what they ARE NOT! They are not money, they are debt!

Mistake #3:
The Practice We Follow

A third mistake I see that has created problems for credit card users is the manner in which the debt is paid off. This can, in fact, be as much of a problem in the long run as the initial over-use of them. There are two common practices that get people into trouble.

FOCUSING ON THE MINIMUM PAYMENT

The payment you are asked to make on your monthly credit card bills is based on a percentage of the balance owed. The monthly statement request is usually around 2% of the existing balance. So, if your existing balance is $1,000, the monthly payment requirement is $20. If your balance is $3,000, the monthly payment requirement is $60. This percentage requirement may vary from card to card, but only slightly.

The problem here comes in to play because most people will determine whether or not they can afford something by how much the monthly minimum payment will be. And why is that a problem, you ask? Let's say you decide you can afford a $3,000 computer because the monthly payment on your card is around $60. If you are 30 years old when you buy the computer, and your interest rate is 17%, and you faithfully pay the required minimum each month, and you are never late, you will be 43 years old when you make your final payment! That's right, it takes 13 years to pay off a $3,000 credit card debt at monthly minimum payments, plus you have also paid $2,600 interest! That's $5,600 for a $3,000 computer over 13 years. That can't be a good way to do business.

Determining what you can afford by focusing on the monthly minimum

payment is not a true perspective. Credit cards require such a small monthly payment that they create the illusion that you are wealthier than you actually are. You may end up buying something that you cannot afford, and paying for it for 15-20 years. Remember, we are not talking about buying a house here, we are talking about buying "stuff" like clothes, food, gas, gifts, etc., that will be long gone before they are even half paid for!

A college freshman told me that when she got her first credit card she rationalized, "Why shouldn't I go out and put $2,500 on my card? I can afford $50 a month," and she did just that! By focusing on the minimum payment instead of the entire debt, she over-extended herself and created the illusion she could afford to spend $2,500 when she could not.

Advertisers lead us to purchase most things today by focusing on the monthly minimum payment. People buy cars that they cannot afford by paying for them for 5-6 years instead of 3 years. Then they end up being "upside-down" on the car loan for a number of years, because they owe more on the car than it is worth. Better hope they don't have to get rid of it, because they can lose a lot of money selling it or trading it in. The buyer or the dealer is not interested in how much is owed on the car, only in what the car is worth. If one owes $10,000 on a car that is only worth $7,000, there is conceivably a lot of money to be lost!

So, think through the debt before you create it. Being able to handle the monthly minimum payment does not mean you can afford it. You may over-extend yourself in debt very quickly if you focus on the minimum payment instead of considering the entire debt itself.

BORROWING TO PAY DEBT

The old adage "You cannot borrow your way to prosperity" is true. And from what I see each day, "Borrowing to pay off credit" works no better. It is like digging a hole in our front yard to fill in the hole in our back yard.

The two most common ways that people try to borrow to pay off their debt is by consolidation loans and home equity loans. It is true that either method will supply enough money to pay off credit card debt, but unless the spending habits of the individual change, it will have no lasting effect upon his financial well being. It merely provides a "quick fix" and within a couple of years his card balances will be back up again.

The home equity loan can even be a worse decision. Equity is the difference between what you owe on your house and what it is worth. For example, if your house is appraised at $100,000 and you owe $80,000 on it, it has $20,000 worth of equity in it that you can borrow against. The problem is that you turn an unsecured debt, like a credit card debt, into a secured debt, and that is rarely a good idea. It may well put your only nestegg, your house, at risk if you cannot make the payments.

Again, the problem most often in having the debt to begin with is bad spending habits. Many people over-extended themselves and go into debt more than they should. That is the problem that must be addressed if any permanent solution is to be found. Borrowing to pay off credit most often just adds to the problem, as the hole of debt is made deeper.

"HAVING MONEY WITH THE MONEY YOU HAVE" definitely involves learning how to manage your credit. Let's summarize what we have learned thus far.

ONE MORE TIME ...

Why Do Most People Run Into Problems With Credit Cards?

1. The POTENTIAL of getting credit cards is too great. It is simply too easy to over-use them.

2. The PERCEPTION most of us have toward credit cards is that they are money or wealth. They are instead debt.

3. The PRACTICE of borrowing to pay off credit card debt rarely works. It is a quick fix that does not address the main problem, which is poor spending habits. Now, before we leave the subject of credit cards, I went to familiarize you with some credit card terminology and give you some pointers on how to shop for a card.

Credit Card Lingo

ANNUAL MEMBERSHIP FEES: A cost you will pay for the privilege of having that particular card, usually $20-$25 per year.

APR: Annual Percentage Rate, meaning the rate of interest you will pay on the purchases you make.

CASH ADVANCE: Actual cash you can receive from an ATM, or other bank transaction, by using your card. The amount is charged to your card. The interest rate for cash advances is usually higher than for other purchases, and is the last thing to be paid off on your card balance.

CONVENIENCE CHECK: This looks similar to a check, but is merely a marketing tool from your credit card company to make it convenient for you to take out a cash advance on your credit card.

CREDIT LIMIT: The amount you can purchase on the card, its buying power; $4,000 is an average credit limit today.

DEBIT CARD: A card that can withdraw the purchase amount directly from your checking account without a separate billing from the card company. The withdrawal is often immediate.

GRACE PERIOD: The number of days you have to pay off your purchases in full without incurring a finance charge (interest charge).

INTRODUCTORY RATE: A special "teaser rate" of interest offered to the prospective cardholder. The lower rate is offered for the first 6-9 months and then jumps to the normal rate.

LATE FEE: The amount you are charged for not getting your payment in on time, usually $20–$29.

OVER-LIMIT FEE: The amount you are charged for charging more than your credit limit allows, usually $20–$29.

PRE-APPROVED: You will get the card if you apply for it.

SECURED CARD: A card that requires a cash security deposit to reduce the amount of risk to the bank, usually offered to those with little credit history or bad credit.

SHOPPING FOR A CREDIT CARD

Subtitle: Read The Fine Print

1. Compare the Annual Percentage Rates (APR).

2. Get a credit limit higher than you need. On the pre-approved promotions remember the words "up to" such an amount, does not necessarily mean you will be granted the highest amount.

3. See if a security deposit is required.

4. Avoid cards with Annual Membership Fees. You can usually find a card with no annual membership fee.

5. Look for an introductory interest rate card.

6. See if there are any "perks" to having and using the card. Such things as "cash back" (a percentage of your total purchase amount paid back to you by the bank), frequent-flyer miles credit, discounts on cruises, lodging, or gifts etc., are frequent bonuses offered to those who will order a card.

7. See what the required monthly minimum payment percent age is. A payment of 2% of the existing balance is average.

8. See what the length of the grace period is.

9. See if you can transfer existing credit card balances at the introductory or reduced rate of interest.

10. Compare late fee and over limit fee information.

JOB INCOME

The most common type of income is that derived from a job. Look at this amount in terms of net income, or "take home" pay. This is the actual amount of money you receive after taxes and other deductions are taken out of your check.

What is your average net income each pay period? $_____

Next, figure your monthly "take home" pay. This is done by multiplying your average take home pay by the number of times you are paid in a year. Then, divide that amount by 12. For example, if you are paid weekly, multiply your take home pay by 52 (weekly pay periods), then divide by 12 (months). If you are paid every two weeks, multiply by 26 then divide by 12. If you are paid twice a month (i.e., the 1st and 15th) simply multiply your take home pay by 2. Or, if you are paid once a month, you already have a monthly figure.

So, what is your average monthly income from your job? (Be sure to include all income earners who are helping pay expenses) $_____

ONE MORE TIME ...

Average Monthly Take Home = Take Home Per Pay Period X Number of Pay Periods Per Year ÷ 12.

If Paid Weekly: Net $ Per Pay Period X 52 ÷ 12.
If Paid Bi-Weekly: Net $ Per Pay Period X 26 ÷ 12.
If Paid Twice a Month: Net $ Per Pay Period X 2
If Paid Monthly: You Already Have The Figure

OTHER INCOME

It is also necessary for us to consider any other sources of income you may have. Consider this list of sources and see if any applies to you:

PART-TIME JOB $ _____
MILITARY $ _____
CHILD SUPPORT $ _____
SOCIAL SECURITY $ _____
DISABILITY $ _____
INVESTMENT INCOME $ _____
OTHER INCOME $ _____

TOTAL AVERAGE MONTHLY INCOME

Now add together all the totals from all sources of income. This amount is your average monthly income. $ _____

Step 2: YOUR PATTERN OF SPENDING

The next step in setting up a workable budget is to determine what your average monthly expenses are. If you use a checkbook, many of your expenses will be recorded there. You can simply go through your checkbook ledger and record the past expenses. But there are numerous "cash" purchases that are not recorded. These need to be known too. They can really add up over a month's time. You can either take an "educated guess" at what you are spending in cash amounts, or you may want to "journal" your expenses for 4-6 weeks. This is done by purchasing a small pocket notepad and writing down everything you spend. This little book becomes a "journal" of your expenses. At month's end, go through it and write down the amount totals for the different types of things you bought. Journaling is a real "eye opener" for most of us.

CONVERTING YOUR EXPENSES

Some expenses are not incurred every month. They may occur quarterly or semi-annually like car insurance. Other expenses are incurred sporadically like clothing purchases or video rentals. To better understand your pattern of spending, convert all your expenses to monthly averages. This is done in one of two ways.

If the expense is incurred less than once a month, determine how many times it occurs in a year and divide that number by 12. For example, Joe's car insurance is paid quarterly. If his quarterly premium is $270, his monthly average is $90 ($270 X 4 = $1,080; $1,080 ÷ 12 = $90).

Other expenses occur more than once per month such as a weekly expense. To determine the monthly average, multiply the expense by the number of times it occurs each month. For example, Barry's weekly giving to church is $5. His monthly average is $20 ($5 X 4 = $20).

ONE MORE TIME ...

To determine the monthly average of expenses occurring less than once per month, divide the yearly expense total by 12.

For those occurring more than once a month, multiply the expense times the number of occurrences per month.

CATEGORIZING YOUR EXPENSES

The following chart has been prepared to help you group your monthly expenses into categories. Notice that the list is divided into two general kinds of expenses: FIXED and FLEXIBLE. A FIXED expense is constant in its frequency and amount. These expenses are often the most important expenses and are not easy to change. They are the "have to" instead of the "want to" type. A car payment is a good example of a FIXED expense. FIXED expenses usually reflect areas of commitment.

A FLEXIBLE expense fluctuates in its frequency and amount. It is a bit easier to change, and it usually is not quite as important or necessary as a FIXED expense. Entertainment would be a good example of a FLEXIBLE expense.

Before filling out the chart, it may help you to know the national averages for a couple of the categories. Your personal expense may be higher or lower than average, so don't worry if your expense is different. The national averages just give you an approximate standard to go by. The national average for car upkeep is around $50 per month ($600 per year). This is because your car will probably need tires, brakes, or exhaust every three years, and each averages about $400. The national average for clothing expense ranges from $25-$50 per person per month ($300-$600 per year). Most other expenses are pretty much on an individual basis.

So, let's go through the list and mark your average monthly expense in each category. After you are done, total each category and add all the totals together. This amount is your average monthly expense total.

16

AVERAGE MONTHLY EXPENSE LIST

FIXED EXPENSES:

HOUSING
Rent or Mortgage _____
2nd Mortgage or Lot Rent _____
Energy (Gas,Oil,Propane,Elect.) _____
Water, Trash _____
Phone/Cell/Internet _____
Cable/Satellite _____
Home Maintenance & Repair _____
Property Taxes (if not in payment) _____
Insurance _____

FOOD AND SUNDRIES
Groceries _____
Laundry Items _____
Baby Supplies _____
Personal Items (Wal-Mart, K-Mart) _____

AUTO EXPENSES
Payment _____
Insurance _____
Gas _____
Upkeep _____
License Plates _____

MEDICAL EXPENSES
Insurance (Unless Deducted) _____
Doctor/Dentist _____
Pharmacy _____

MISCELLANEOUS
Day Care _____
Child Support _____
Student Loans _____
Credit Cards _____
Other Loans _____
Tuition & Books _____
Savings _____
Other _____
Other _____

TOTAL FIXED EXPENSES _____

FLEXIBLE EXPENSES

Clothing_____
Laundry_____
Dry Cleaning_____
Lunches_____
Work/School_____
Travel_____
Vacations_____
Misc._____
Church_____
Pets_____
Newspaper_____
Barber_____
Alcohol_____
Tobacco_____
Gambling_____
Gifts (include Xmas
Entertainment /
Meals out_____
Health Club /YMCA_____
Lessons_____
Other_____
Other_____
Other_____

**TOTAL FLEXIBLE
EXPENSES**_____

COMPARING INCOME AND EXPENSES

It is important at this point to stop a minute and see how you have been doing in your money management. Which is greater each month, your income or your expenses? The answer is seen by subtracting your total average monthly expense from your total average monthly income. This amount is your cash flow.

CASH FLOW

	$_____	Average Monthly Income
Minus	$_____	Average Monthly Expenses
Equals	$_____	Average Monthly Cash Flow

Is your cash flow a positive or negative number? In other words, have you been spending more or less than you make? If your cash flow is positive, congratulations! You have been living within your means. You may want to make some adjustments in your budget, but overall you have been doing well.

But if you find that you have been spending more than you make, it's time to get to work right away. No one can survive long financially when his cash flow is negative. Spending more than you make will dig a hole of debt very quickly that can literally take years from which to recover. CHANGE must be considered: either spend less, make more, or a combination of both.

CHANGING OUR HABITS

This is a crucial step in setting up a budget, because without making needed changes you will fall short of accomplishing your goal. To stop short of actually adjusting income/expenses is similar to driving a car by looking in the rearview mirror; you only see where you have been, not where you want to go. Changes will allow you to chart the course for the future. But how do you make changes?

18

Looking for changes is the starting point. Considering these questions will allow you to see if changes are indeed needed:

Are monthly expenses more than monthly income? Y____ N____
Are there areas where you want to spend less?   Y____ N____
Are there areas where you want to spend more?   Y____ N____
Is savings an area that you have neglected?   Y____ N____

If you answered "yes" to any of the questions, we need to work on some changes in your spending habits. And how is that accomplished?

Making changes is accomplished by going through the Average Monthly Expense List again and adjusting the amounts in the individual categories. This time use a different colored pen and write in the new amount next to the old one. The new amount reflects what you **should** be doing instead of what you have been doing. The new amount could be more or less than the old depending upon why you are making the changes. If your cash flow was negative, then your new amounts must total less than they did before.

Re-add your totals and see how your projected expenses now compare to your income each month. Do you now have a positive cash flow? Did you include an amount for savings each month (shoot for a balance in your savings account of 1-1/2 times your monthly income)? Do the amounts now reflect a responsible management of your money? Are you satisfied with what you see?

Step 3: YOUR PERSPECTIVE

Knowing about and making needed changes in your spending habits are very important steps in setting up a budget, but there is another matter that is of equal importance. That is the issue of how you view your money in regard to your perspective toward it. This will be a governing factor as to whether you have control over it, or it has control over you! Let me illustrate. Below are two pies of exactly the some size.

Julie's Pie: Sliced   Sarah's Pie: Whole

The first is cut into slices and the second one is whole. Julie has guests coming for dinner and she wants to be sure everyone has a piece of pie. She sliced her pie and now views it as designated pieces, each piece reserved for one of her guests. Again, both pies have the same amount of pie, only one is viewed as a number of designated slices, while the other is viewed in terms of the whole amount.

DOES PERSPECTIVE MATTER?

The Whole   Sliced into Pieces

Now, let's say that you look at your money in the same perspective that Julie looked at her pie. Instead of seeing your money as one whole amount, try to visualize it as individual pieces which are designated for individual expense

categories. In other words, "slice" it up and reserve each slice for its intended purpose. The slice designated for the car payment is reserved for that purpose; the slice designated for savings is reserved for that purpose; the slice designated for clothing is reserved for that purpose. Every slice is designated for an intended use. How would this perspective make things better for you financially?

Jerry is a guy who works hard in retail sales. He makes pretty good money, but never seems to have enough to go around. He views his money in terms of the whole amount in his billfold or his checkbook. One Saturday afternoon he receives a call from his friend George with an invitation. "Hey, Jerry, a group of us are going for pizza and a movie tonight. Got any money? Want to go?" Jerry looks in his billfold and sees he has $65. "Sure, I have plenty of money! What time?" Now, there is nothing wrong with Jerry going with his friends except his car payment of $140 is due next week and he has nothing saved back for it. Guess he will be a few days late on the car payment again!

Then there is Mitch who works in a factory and also makes pretty good money. He has a different perspective of his money. He sees it like a sliced-up pie with each piece reserved for an intended use. He also received a call from George on Saturday afternoon and he too, agreed to accept the invitation. But he did so knowing that his car payment would be paid on time. He had been setting aside a portion of his income for it, just like reserving a piece of pie for a guest. His "yes" answer was based on another slice of his income that was designated "Entertainment." He had enough money in that "slice" to go for pizza and a movie. Interestingly enough, Mitch makes just about the some amount of money as does Jerry, and his expenses are also very similar. It is their perspective toward their money that seems to make the difference as to whether or not they have control over their money or it over them.

Perspective DOES make a difference because it determines how you handle the money you make. If you view your money in one lump sum, you will likely spend money for something that should instead be set aside for another soon-to-be-due obligation. This results in a failure to meet your payment deadlines on time. So, starting right now, try to cultivate a perspective toward your money as though you had sliced it into pieces that are designated for intended purposes. This perspective, and a little planning, will enable you to pay your bills on time, plus, have money to do extra things too.

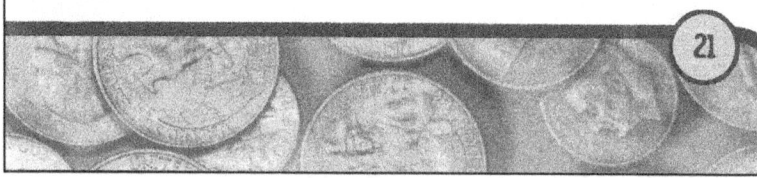

21

TIME OUT FOR REFLECTION

Sit back for just a minute and reflect on what you have done so far. You have determined your PAY (Average Monthly Income), and you have compared it to your PATTERN OF SPENDING (Average Monthly Expenses). Then we discussed our PERSPECTIVE, and how important it is to view our money as though it were a pie sliced into designated pieces. Now it's time to move into the last step of developing a workable budget. It is a step that will tie all of our previous work together. It will move us from "paperwork to practice!"

Step 4: YOUR PLAN

In choosing a plan that will translate your new perspective toward your money into a new practice, I want to offer a very simple approach. The purpose is to teach you a "no-frills" plan, that is, one that is reduced to the lowest common denominator. It will be easy for you to make it more complex once you understand how it works. But that is OK. Budgets must be "custom-made" if they are to "fit" real life situations.

This plan will require you to have two things: (1) a checking account and (2) a number of business-size envelopes. For those of you who do not have a checking account, you may use a savings account instead. One of the two is needed to avoid large sums of cash lying around the house. The basic plan here is to pay your FIXED expenses from your checking (savings) account, and your FLEX-IBLE expenses from cash in your envelopes. Let's see how the plan is set up.

FIRST: Go back to the work you did on the Average Monthly Expense List and write down the amount you have for your total FIXED expenses $_____. It is this amount that must be deposited into your checking account (or savings account) each month so you can be sure to meet your obligations. The money in this account is **only** for FIXED expenses. Picture a pie with a large piece cut out of it. The pie **remaining** in the pie pan symbolizes your FIXED expenses, which will be paid from your checking or savings. The rest of the pie is for your FLEXIBLE expenses, which we will talk about in a minute.

To determine how much *out of each check* must be set aside for your

FIXED expenses, divide the total monthly amount needed by the number of times you are paid each month.

For example, if your FIXED expenses total $1,000 per month and you are paid weekly, then $250 must go from each paycheck to your checking (savings) account. If you are paid bi-weekly or if you are paid twice per month, then $500 per pay period must go to your checking (savings) account.

By now, some of you have discovered a "snag." You have two income earners, but the two incomes are not the same. One is more than the other. How do you determine how much each pays when the paychecks are different? The amount taken from each wage earner depends upon what percentage their individual income is of the total income earned.

Let me illustrate. Joe and Jan need to put $2,100 a month toward FIXED expenses. Joe brings in $1,500 per month while his wife, Jan, brings home $1,000 per month. Jan's income is 40% of the total income earned ($1000 ÷ $2500 = 40%). So the amount taken from her checks will represent 40% of the total amount needed. Joe's portion will equal 60% of the amount needed ($1,500 ÷ $2,500 = 60%). In dollar amounts that would equal $840 from Jan (40% of $ 2,100) and $1260 from Joe (60% of $ 2,100).

ONE MORE TIME ...

To determine what portion each wage earner pays from his check, figure what percentage his income is of the total income earned. Multiply that percentage by the total amount needed, and that dollar amount equals his share of contribution.

If the dollar amount of the highest wage earner is close to the total amount needed for FIXED expenses, it is sometimes just as easy to designate that income for FIXED expense and the other for FLEXIBLE.

SECOND: Next, determine into how many categories to divide your FLEXIBLE expenses. The FLEXIBLE expenses are listed on the average monthly expense list already. I would suggest using maybe five or six envelopes, but whatever suits your needs is best.

After you have grouped your FLEXIBLE expenses into categories, write the NAME of the category on each envelope. At the beginning, you may also want to list the specific expenses in that category on the outside of the envelope too, just so you remember what is included in that category.

Now, write on the envelope the total amount of money needed per month for each category. These totals may be taken from the work you have already done on the average monthly expense list.

Last of all, determine how much money you must put in each envelope each paycheck to equal the total amount needed at month's end. Again, this is done by dividing the total amount needed by the number of pay periods per month. And if there is more than one wage earner, use the percentage method (explained on the previous page) to calculate how much comes out of each wage earner's check each pay period.

ANTICIPATED PROBLEM!

Since you will not start this program with envelopes full of money, you may find that a bill is due before you have enough accumulated to pay it. What do you do? Simply borrow from yourself and pay it back next payday! That is, find a category that is not due right now, and transfer the money to the category that is due. But, remember to pay yourself back or you will come up short in that category from which you borrowed.

ONE MORE TIME ...

(1) Total your FIXED expenses for the month and divide this amount by the number of pay periods per month. This amount is deposited into your checking account or savings account each pay period. FIXED expenses are paid from this account.

(2) Determine how many envelopes you will use for FLEXIBLE expenses. Label each and determine how much money goes into each envelope per pay period.

(3) Pay FIXED expenses out of your checking account (or savings account) and FLEXIBLE expenses with cash from your envelopes.

(4) If you are short in your checkbook or in a specific envelope, borrow from yourself temporarily and then pay yourself back next pay period.

Don't be discouraged the first few months. No matter how you first set up your personal budget, it will take time to fine tune it. Experiment with it until you find a plan that works for you. The specific plan is not the important thing. As you cultivate the ability to see your income in light of your expenses, the plan will merely be a tool to translate that perspective into real life practice!

You can "HAVE MONEY WITH THE MONEY YOU HAVE," but you must be willing to invest a bit of time and effort initially. Learning to manage your credit and your cash is certainly within your reach. Implementing the principles you have just learned will bring about changes in your financial well-being that can last you a lifetime. Try them and see. The principles will work if you will work them.

What People Are Saying About Jim Garnett, The Debt Doctor

"As a guest lecturer at Iowa State University, Jim did a wonderful job of keeping the students engaged. He understands what the students need to know and presents it in a manner that is easy to understand. I plan on having Jim back." **Doug Brokowski, Director of the Iowa State University Financial Counseling Clinic, Ames**

"Many thanks to Jim Garnett for taking the time to put together this extremely well-written financial booklet. He not only has a knack for explaining himself clearly, but can do so with humor." **Mary Jo Meeks, CEO United Service Credit Union, Des Moines**

"Mr. Garnett spoke to my Personal Finance class and the Economics class at Twin Cedars. His power point presentation on credit cards was awesome. The graphics and examples were perfect for our High School students, who will be receiving credit card offers in the mail any day now. He used stories and scenarios involving the kids and relating to their experiences, and they were listening intently to him the entire hour." **Donna Huston, Business Teacher, Twin Cedars Community Schools**

"Jim has visited my class multiple times for presentations, and my students are always rewarded with a new perspective on managing their personal finances. His presentations are enjoyable and informative. Most of all, I believe that he has an impact in helping students understand the importance of avoiding debt, which is so prevalent among many college-age students today." **Brad Duerson, Professor of Economics, DMACC, Ankeny Campus**

"My thanks to Jim Garnett for the numerous student seminars and books he has provided for our AIB College of Business students. Jim is not only a dynamic speaker, but he has the ability to reach college students with his valuable message. He incorporates real life situations, consequences, and solutions into his presentations. Evaluations prove that our students are taking his information and putting it to practical use." **Sheila Keene, M.S., L.M.H.C., Director of Student Counseling, AIB College of Business**

"Jim's message on financial literacy and wellness provides a refreshing dose of reality for individuals from all walks of life and presents tangible strategies to improve their financial practices." **Brad L. Spielman, Adjunct Instructor, Department of Student Development, DMACC Urban Campus**

"The nonprofit Institute of Consumer Financial Education has utilized the financial savvy of Jim Garnett in a variety of ways over the past years. Jim is a charter member of the ICFE's Board of Educational Advisors. We have published over 30 of Jim's articles on our web pages and in eNEWS broadcasts, and host his AskMrG Education Library on two of our websites. Jim is an accomplished platform presenter and makes financial education fun." **Paul Richard, Executive Director, Institute of Consumer Financial Education, San Diego, Ca 92163**

Jim Garnett is a much sought-after speaker, counselor, and author. After 30 years of family and financial counseling, he has affectionately earned the title The Debt Doctor. He also is a Nationally Certified Parent Trainer and over the last 15 years has conducted over 750 Smart Discipline Seminars across the State of Iowa. You may contact him at askmrg@yahoo.com or check out his websites at:
AskMrG.Com
SmartDiscipline.Info